the lost

BETRAYAL, KARMA AND FALL

FATIMA AMIN

Epigraph

"In the ashes of betrayal, we find the truth of our fall;
For every wound inflicted, karma waits, its reckoning
sure."

Contents

Part 2: The Karma

Foreword

"The Lost - Betrayal, Karma, and Fall" explores the deep effects of betrayal, the inevitable pull of karma, and the fall that follows. Through these poems, I examine the raw emotions of betrayal—anger, sorrow, and regret—and the truth that every action has its consequences. This collection reminds us that while karma can be harsh, it seeks balance and ultimately leads to growth.

Within these verses, you will find both the pain of loss and the quiet hope that rises from it. This journey is not just about falling, but about rising again.

Preface

Writing "The Lost - Betrayal, Karma, and Fall" was a journey through the raw emotions that follow betrayal. Betrayal shakes the core of who we are, leaving us vulnerable and lost. This collection reflects the pain of that experience and the inevitable forces of karma that follow.

Each poem explores moments of anger, regret, and loss, but also the quiet understanding that karma brings balance. No action goes without consequence, and sometimes the fall is just the beginning of something new.

Through these verses, I hope to offer a reminder that even in the darkest moments, there is room for growth, healing, and reflection. For anyone who has faced betrayal or the weight of their own actions, this book seeks to provide a sense of shared experience and hope.

Introduction

"The Lost - Betrayal, Karma, and Fall" is a collection that explores the complexities of human emotions; the pain of betrayal, the weight of karma, and the inevitable fall that follows. This book is not just a journey through raw emotions, but also an exploration of various literary forms to capture the depth of these themes.

The collection weaves together poems, ode, elegy, limericks, free verse, ballads, chinquapin, haiku, satirical poetry, prose, and epistolary poetry.

Each form serves a distinct purpose, offering a unique perspective and voice on the experiences of loss, reckoning, and transformation. From the rhythmic flow of ballads to the sharpness of satire, these forms enrich the narrative and bring the themes to life in multifaceted ways.

Every piece in this book speaks to those who have felt the sting of betrayal, faced the consequences of their actions, or experienced the weight of the fall. It is a reminder that even in our darkest moments, there is room for growth, understanding, and, eventually, redemption.

(The Betrayal)

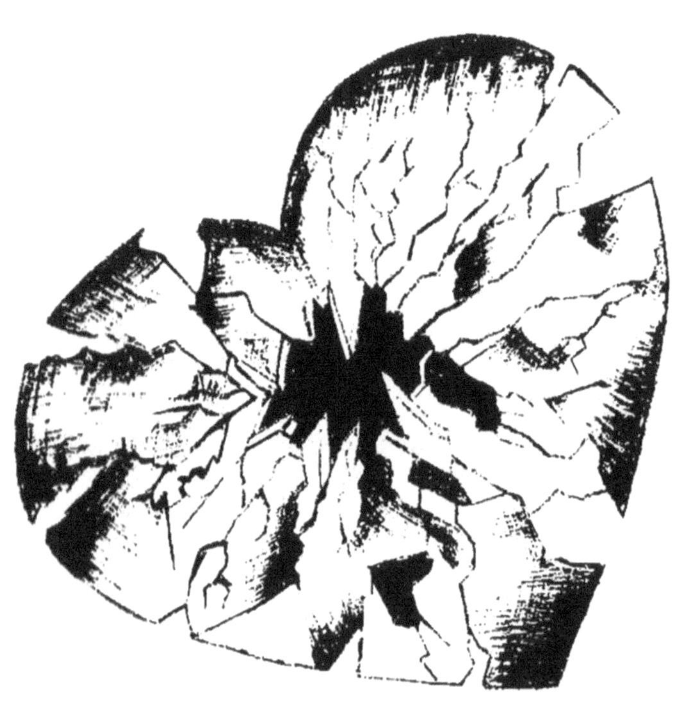

1. The Knife That Smiled

Beneath the veil of charm so bright,
a shadow danced in soft moonlight.
A voice so sweet, a touch so kind,
Yet secrets lingered, sharp and blind.

eyes like mirrors, they drew me near,
reflecting trust, erasing fear.
A hand extended, warm and mild,
but hid within—a knife that smiled.

Its blade was forged in whispered lies,
in promises and alibis.
It gleamed beneath the cloak of grace,
Its cut concealed by a friendly face.

I leaned on words, I drank the tune,
not knowing trust would sour too soon.
The laughter sang, the bond beguiled,
yer all the while, the knife had smiled.

Oh, lesson learned, though scars remain,
the cost of love, the weight of pain.
Beware the warmth that seems beguiled,
for sharpest wounds come from the knife that
smiled.

Let this be marked in shadows deep,
a warning carved where truths must sleep.
Not all who shine are undefiled—
beware the knife that softly smiled.

2. Echoes of Trust

Quiet halls hold the weight of grief,
aching beneath the stolen belief.
Promises whispered, soft and sweet,
now lie shattered at my feet.

Your words once wove a brilliant thread,
binding dreams where hope had fled.
But threads can snap, and truths unwind,
leaving scars both cruel and unkind.

Laughter fades to a hollow tune,
a mournful echo beneath the moon.
Each vow you broke, a wound unhealed,
a silent scream the dark concealed.

The soul still aches for what was lost,
a heavy heart bears love's true cost.
Trust, once given, cannot return,
its ashes smolder, forever burning.

So here I stand in the shadow's dust
haunted still by the echoes of trust.

3. Glass Hearts, Shattered

A heart so fragile, clear as glass,
held in hands that let it pass.
It gleamed with trust, a tender light,
but you turned day into night.

Your words were petals, soft and fair,
yet thorns lay hidden, unaware.
I opened wide, let the truth unfold,
not knowing your touch would be so cold.

You pressed too hard, the cracks began,
a fault line carved by careless hands.
Each promise made, each lie concealed,
splintered the love I once revealed.

Pieces fell with a haunting chime,
moments lost to the edge of time.
The shards reflected what could not stay,
dreams scattered in disarray.

Now I gather the fragments near,
cut by memories sharp and clear.
No mending glue, no gentle art,
can heal the wounds of a glass heart.

Yet still I rise, though broken, scarred,
stronger now, though love was marred.
For even shattered, I am whole,
a tempered spirit, a resilient soul.

4. Poison in the Wine

Ruby,
a shining lure
sweet lies in every drop—
betrayal cloaked in celebration,
Venom.

5. The Judas Among us

Beneath the sun's once faithful glow,
a shadow walked where trust should grow.
A friend, a brother, a bond we praised,
now torn apart in a treacherous blaze.

You sat among us, hand in hand,
shared our dreams, our hopes, our plans.
Your smile, a mask, your words, a snare,
a serpent hidden in the lion's lair.

How bitter the knife that finds its mark,
when wielded by one who shared our spark.
Your touch was warm, your eyes sincere,
yet lies were all you held so near.

The table where we broke our bread,
now bears the weight of words unsaid.
The wine we sipped to seal our trust,
turns sour now in grief and dust.

Oh, Judas cloaked in love's disguise,
What did you gain through our demise?
A fleeting coin, a hollow prize,
while we are left with haunted cries.

Still, the wound will heal with time's embrace,
though scars remain to mark your face.
For even in betrayal's sting,
The truth will rise on a steadfast wing.

And as we mourn what we have lost,
we'll learn the price of trust's great cost.
The Judas among us may yet fall,
but love endures beyond it all.

6. Silence Screams Too

Ah!, the noble art of saying naught
a silent blade so deftly wrought
No word was spoken, no vow betrayed
Yet guilt drips thick from those who stayed.

You sat and watched the world ignite
a quiet spectator to the fight
nor a murmur, not a sound
yet your stillness burned the ground.

Such valor in your muted stance
the hero of a stolen chance
a statue carved from hollow stone
while others bled, you stood alone.

"Not my place," your anthem rang
a choir of cowards where justice hangs
the silence roared, it screamed, it cried
with every truth you left to die.

Oh!, champions of the quiet way
how loudly your inaction plays
for betrayal hides not in a shout
but in the whispers you leave out.

So raise a glass to quiet's throne
where guilt and apathy are sewn
the silence screams, it always will
a traitor's voice, deafening still.

7. Behind Closed Doors

Behind Closed Doors
whispers in the dark,
shadows cradle hidden lies
Truth is left to fade.

8. The Web They Wove

Silent threads spun, soft and tight,
a web of lies concealed from sight.
Whispers tangled in every strand,
a truth twisted by a steady hand.

Promises forged in shadow's glow,
bound by secrets none could know.
Each word a trap, each glance a chain,
the web they wove in silent pain.

Gentle hands that shaped the lie,
underneath a watchful eye.
Every smile, a thin disguise,
hiding the deceit in their eyes.

A dance of trust, a fleeting grace,
each step concealed a darker place.
The web expanded, never slow,
built on the lies they chose to sow.

Falsehoods bloomed in quiet hours,
weakened hearts, unseen powers.
Still, the web they wove remained,
a prison formed, a soul restrained.

But time will break the threads apart,
revealing lies that once held heart.
The web will fall, the truth will show,
exposing all the pain they sowed.

9. *Whispers of the Fallen*

Beneath the moon, a shadow cries
the whispers of the fallen rise.
Voices lost, forgotten, cold
tales of betrayal, never told
They walked with trust, their hearts laid bare
unseen the knives that waited there.
Each smile a lie, each word a snare
left broken dreams scattered in despair.

"We gave our all, we stood beside,"
The voices wail, a mournful tide.
"But in the dark, our love was sold,
For empty promises, for hearts grown cold."
Betrayed by those who swore to stay,
Their souls now drift, led far away.
A bond once strong, now turned to rust,
Crushed beneath the weight of trust.

"We lived in shadows, hearts concealed,
Until the truth could be revealed.
But silence spoke, and so we fell,
Forgotten in a twisted spell."
In every whisper, sorrow sings,
Of shattered hopes and broken wings.

The fallen speak with voices clear,
Yet no one listens, none draws near.

"Remember us, remember well,
The price we paid, the tales we tell.
For in the end, when all is done,
We were the lost, the silenced ones."
So listen close, and hear their call,
The whispers rise, the shadows fall.

For in the silence of the night,
The fallen speak of lost delight.

10. The Mirage of Loyalty

There once was a trust, bright and clear
that shimmered like gold, far and near.
But as time passed by
I began to believe,
and vanished, just like a mirage, disappeared.

11. Hands That Let Go

Once they held me, strong and tight
now their grip fades into the night.
Promises whispered, soft and slow
but when I needed them, they let it go.

12. The Mirror Lies

I looked into the glass,
expecting truth to stare back at me,
but the reflection was not my own.
It wore my face,
spoke my voice,
but its eyes—empty, hollow—
betrayed the soul within.
A thousand whispers echoed,
soft as promises, sharp as knives.
The lies I told myself
twisted and wrapped around my heart,
growing thicker with each passing day.
Who am I now?
This stranger who wears my skin,
who walks my path,
who says the things I dare not believe.
I chased the image for so long,
thinking it was me,
only to find it fading with the light,
a mirage dissolving
into the cold morning air.
The mirror reflects nothing but silence,
and I am left to wonder—
what was truth,
and what was the lie
I became?

13. Thorns among Roses

Thorns Among Roses
We bloom together,
hands entwined in a garden of smiles,
where laughter dances in the air,
and the world sees only petals,
soft and bright,
glimmering in the sun.
But beneath the surface,
hidden in the shade,
there are thorns—
silent, sharp, and waiting.
They prick the skin
when no one looks,
drawing blood from hearts
that once beat in sync.
In the quiet,
the thorns tear at the seams,
unseen, unnoticed,
until the roses wilt,
their colors fading to gray.
The pain grows in the shadows,
masked by beauty,
cloaked in the lies we tell ourselves.
We keep walking through the garden,
careful not to speak of what we feel,

holding tight to the illusion,
because the thorns have become familiar,
and the roses—
they are all we know.

14. The Hourglass of Deceit

Oh Time! thy sands fall slow and sure
Each grain a whisper, soft, demure,
In thy embrace, all truths arise
What once was hidden, now unwise,
The hourglass, so still, so tall
Holds secrets in its fragile call,
What once was masked in velvet lies
Now cracks beneath thy steady sighs,
For in the turning of thy face
Deceit is laid bare, without grace,
A smile once sweet, a hand once kind
Now shows the dark, the twisted mind,
The mask dissolves, the truth does bleed
As time reveals each selfish deed,
What was concealed, now starkly stands
A web of lies, unravelled strands.

Oh Time! thy power none can flee
Thy sands will show what eyes can't see,
For in thy endless, quiet sweep
Betrayal's face, thou shalt keep,
So let the glass turn, let it fall
For truth will rise, despite it all,
The hourglass will claim its due—
And all the lies will fade from view.

15. Ashes of Affection

Once, love burned with fierce desire
A flame that reached, that soared, that spired.
Its warmth a comfort, soft and pure,
A bond we thought would long endure.

But shadows crept where light had been
A whispered word, a hidden sin.
The flames turned cold, the warmth betrayed,
And in its wake, the embers laid.

Now, all that's left are scattered cries
A heart turned cold, beneath dark skies.
The love we held, now turned to dust,
A fleeting spark betrayed by trust.

I gather ashes, soft and still
The remnants of a dream once real.
The pieces fall, like fading light,
A love consumed by endless nights.

The fire's gone, the warmth has fled
And in its place, a soul misled.
What once was bright, now burns away,
Leaving me to mourn the day.

So let the wind carry the past
The shattered love, the final gasp.
For in the ashes, all that's true,
Betrayal left no trace of you.

16. Veins of Treachery

Through veins once pulsing with trust and fire,
Flows now the chill of a toxic mire.
Each beat of the heart, a silent scream,
Echoes the shatter of love's bright dream.

The words you spoke, sweet venom concealed,
Promises forged, yet never revealed.
Your touch, once tender, now burns my skin,
A mark of the treachery buried within.

I offered my soul, my heart laid bare,
But found your truths were never there.
A shadow looms where sunlight played,
In the garden of trust, only thorns remain.

Now I lie still, a ghost of before,
Haunted by whispers of the love I wore.
The poison spreads, relentless and slow,
Turning what thrived into what must go.

Yet in the ruin, a seed may grow,
A quiet strength from this hollowed woe.
For though veins of treachery bleed me dry,
The soul remembers how to survive.

17. Masks That Fit too Well

Oh! crafted masks, so finely made,
With painted smiles that never fade.
You wear them well, a flawless guise,
Deceit concealed in borrowed eyes.

Your words, like honey, softly flow,
Yet hide the sting that lurks below.
A tender hand, a gentle touch,
That wounds the heart it claims so much.

In shadows deep, your truth resides,
Behind the veil where kindness hides.
A friend in name, a foe in deed,
Sowing doubt with every seed.

Yet masks will crack, and truths will bare,
No lie can linger in the air.
For those who feign, the time will tell—
The price of masks that fit too well.

18. *Promises Written in Sand*

Your words fell soft, like morning dew,
A melody of dreams anew.
You swore by stars, by skies, by time,
Each vow a whisper, sweet and sublime.

You painted worlds of love's embrace,
Of endless days, of steady grace.
But beneath the beauty of your tone,
Lurked shadows where the truth was sown.

Each promise carved with fleeting care,
Etched on shores of shifting air.
No anchor held, no roots ran deep,
Just fragile lines the tide would sweep.

The moonlight watched, the waves conspired,
To test the love that once inspired.
And when the waters kissed the sand,
They carried away your gentle hand.

I stood and stared, my heart in flight,
As tides erased what once felt right.
Your words dissolved, their weight was none,
Like ashes scattered in the sun.

For promises written in sand don't stay,
They drift, they vanish, they slip away.
They speak of forever, yet last a breath,
And leave behind the taste of death.

Yet in the ruin, I found my truth,
A lesson carved from fleeting youth:
To trust the hands that hold their ground,
To seek a love where roots are found.

For words that last are forged in stone,
Not borrowed from a moment alone.
The heart remembers, the soul withstands,
But never trusts vows made in sand.

19. Daggers In their Smile

They came with warmth, with words so sweet,
A tender hand, a charm complete.
Their laughter rang like silver chimes,
Concealing shadows in their rhymes.

Their eyes, a mirror of feigned delight,
A polished mask, reflecting light.
Yet behind the glow, a blade would gleam,
Sharp with betrayal, tearing the dream.

Each smile they gave, a hidden sting,
A subtle twist, a venomous ring.
Their kindness, honey laced with spite,
Cut deeper than the darkest night.

The wounds they left were not of skin,
But buried deep, where trust had been.
A jagged edge, a whispered blow,
Invisible scars that will not show.

I held their words, I held their gaze,
Unaware I walked a maze.
Each turn a trap, each step a lie,
Until I fell, too drained to cry.

But smiles can crack, and masks can fall,
Revealing truths that shatter all.
And now I see, through pain's disguise,
The daggers hidden in their eyes.

So guard your heart, and tread with care,
For not all smiles are true and fair.
The softest touch can tear apart,
A hidden blade will scar the heart.

20. The Hollow Embrace

Oh! what warmth your arms professed,
A cradle where my soul could rest.
Yet now I see, beneath the guise,
A gaping void, a field of lies.

You whispered love in practiced tones,
While building thrones of brittle stones.
Your heart, a mirage I couldn't trace,
Your touch—a phantom's cold embrace.

How grand the act, how well you played,
A lover's mask so deftly made.
But in the dark, the truth would creep,
Your love as shallow as your sleep.

What tender lines you did rehearse,
A poet's gift, a liar's curse.
You painted sunsets, bright and red,
But left me holding grey instead.

I laugh now at your hollow art,
The empty room you called a heart.
A masterpiece of air and dust,
Built on the ashes of my trust.

So take a bow, oh, grand charade,
Your hollow embrace, so well displayed.
The pain still stings, but I'll confess—
You taught me love, or something less.

(The Karma)

21. The Boomerang of Choices

Every action flung into the world eventually circles back, striking with a force we often underestimate. At first, we make choices carelessly, as if the consequences are too distant to matter. We speak words we don't think about, take steps we don't second-guess, as if our lives are separate from the ripples we create. The smallest decision, glance, a passing comment, a fleeting promise, can be cast into the air, seemingly weightless, without much thought for what might follow.

But time has a way of drawing the lines between cause and effect. What feels light and insignificant in the moment gains weight, accumulating with each passing day until we find that what we flung out has come back, faster, sharper, and harder than we anticipated. The boomerang of our choices returns when we least expect it, and we are left to face what we put into motion long ago.

We often underestimate how long it takes, or how precisely the world aligns to return our actions. It doesn't forget. It simply waits. The echoes of our choices don't vanish into thin air. They are gathered, threaded into the fabric of our lives, and when the time comes, they circle back with an intensity that demands attention.

We may try to outrun the inevitable, but it finds us anyway. Sometimes, it arrives quietly, a whisper of something we did or said years ago. Other times, it crashes into us with an undeniable force, leaving us stunned, wondering how we ended up in the very place we once feared. The boomerang of our choices doesn't discriminate. It returns to all of us, regardless of intention or ignorance.

In the end, the force of that return is a reminder that every action, no matter how small or fleeting, has weight. The world doesn't forget. And the choices we make—whether to hurt, to help, to leave, to stay— will always find their way back to us, striking with a force we often underestimate.

22. Echoes in the Void

Karma is patient. It does not rush, nor does it forget. It waits, quietly lingering in the spaces between our actions and their consequences, biding its time in the shadows. For a moment, we might believe that the echoes of our choices have been swallowed by the void, lost in the vastness of time. But like a sound that reverberates across an empty canyon, karma returns. It always returns.

In the beginning, its presence is subtle, like a whisper in the dark—almost imperceptible. We carry on, convinced that we've outrun its reach, that the choices we made in haste or selfishness will fade into memory, unnoticed and unpunished. But the universe has a way of keeping score, even when we think we've forgotten the debt.

Then one day, without warning, it comes back. A chance encounter, a word spoken, a moment of vulnerability—and suddenly, it's there, louder than before. The echo of our past reverberates, clearer and more powerful than we could have imagined. The pain we caused, the lies we told, the love we abandoned—

all of it returns, not in the form we expected, but with the same weight we once cast upon others.

Karma doesn't need to scream to make its presence known. It simply waits for the right moment, and when the time is ripe, it sends its message with a force that cannot be ignored. In that instant, we are reminded that the universe does not forget. It holds every word, every action, every moment in balance, and when the echoes return, they demand attention.

What we put into the world, we will one day meet again, sometimes in unexpected ways. The echoes of our choices, once soft and distant, will find their way back to us, louder, clearer, and with a power that cannot be denied. Karma may be patient, but it is also relentless. It waits, always, to return what we have sent into the void.

23. The Unseen Ledger

Life keeps its accounts balanced, though few realize the weight of its invisible ledger. In every moment, every interaction, an entry is made—debts of malice and credits of kindness, all recorded in the silent pages of the Book of Karma. We go about our days, unaware of the subtle balance being struck, the quiet tallying of all we do and say. We may think our actions go unnoticed, that the harm we cause or the good we offer fades into nothingness, but nothing is truly forgotten.

The ledger is never far behind, quietly waiting to record each debit, each credit. When we act out of spite, when we betray trust or speak words that wound, it is as though we've written in invisible ink. At first, it may seem there are no consequences, no reckoning, and the account appears balanced. But the pages of the ledger do not fade. They stay open, waiting for the time when those actions must be answered for. Life has a way of ensuring that balance is restored.

On the other side, kindness doesn't go unnoticed, though it may feel small at the moment. A gentle word, a selfless act, the quiet support we offer—each one is recorded, added to the balance, even if no one sees. These credits may seem insignificant in the grand scheme of things, but they too accumulate, building a foundation that supports us when we need it most. The ledger of life is never empty, no matter how we try to escape it.

The Book of Karma does not operate in immediate terms. It does not demand an instant return on every choice we make, but rather trusts in the balance of time. What we send into the world, good or ill, is always accounted for, though the reckoning may come in ways we cannot predict. The ledger will be balanced, inevitably.

In the end, we find that life's true currency is neither wealth nor power, but the energy we contribute to the world—our kindness and malice alike. We are all writing in this invisible book, and though we may not see the pages, they are being filled with every breath we take, every decision we make. Life keeps its accounts balanced, and sooner or later, those pages will reveal the truth.

24. Garden of Consequences

We plant the seeds of our deeds in the quiet soil of time—some intentionally, others without thought. Each action, whether good or bad, is a seed we push into the earth, expecting nothing or everything, depending on the moment. These seeds lie hidden for a while, dormant beneath the surface, until time stirs them into growth. Slowly, roots take hold, and the consequences of our choices begin to rise, whether we're ready or not.

Some seeds sprout into flowers—soft, bright, and fragrant. These are the kind words spoken, the selfless acts done without expectation. The flowers bloom into beauty, a reflection of the care we've given to others. The harvest, when it arrives, is sweet and full of joy, a reminder that good intentions and actions create something positive, even if the rewards take time.

Other seeds grow into thorns, sharp and cruel. These are the moments of betrayal, of selfishness, of harm caused without thought. The thorns twist and claw their way upward, a reminder that our darker actions are never truly hidden. They emerge from places we tried to forget or ignore, only to return, relentless and biting. The harvest, though delayed, is inevitable and bitter, a direct consequence of the damage we've wrought.

The garden doesn't judge. It doesn't decide what should bloom. It simply reflects what we plant. The flowers and thorns, bright and painful, are the inevitable result of what we sow. The harvest always comes, whether we're ready to face it or not. We cannot escape the consequences of our actions. They are the fruit of the seeds we've planted, and we must live with what we've grown, sweet or bitter.

25. The Spider's Web

We weave our own entanglements, each thread spun with intention or carelessness, creating a complex design of our own making. At first, the web seems harmless, a delicate pattern, almost invisible, stretching out around us. It's easy to think that we are in control, crafting a structure that serves our needs, trapping nothing more than the small, fleeting moments of life. We move through it effortlessly, believing that the threads are light and fragile, unaware of the weight they'll soon carry.

Each choice we make is a strand added to the web. A lie whispered here, a promise broken there, a selfish act or an unkind word. Each moment, each decision, contributes to the web's growth, a pattern forming that we cannot always see. We don't notice how the threads begin to intertwine, how they slowly become tighter and more complex until we find ourselves caught in our own creation.

Karma watches, always patient, always waiting. It sees the web grow, sees the strands weave together, and knows that eventually, we will struggle to break free. The web we've made, once light and seemingly harmless, will turn on us, binding us in the very threads we spun. We fight against it, confused by the sudden weight, the tightness that wasn't there before. But karma has already been here, silently observing, knowing that the entanglements we've created are the result of our own actions.

We struggle, pulling at the threads, trying to free ourselves, unaware that with every movement, we only make the web tighter. The more we resist, the more trapped we become. It's a dance we can't escape, a struggle we can't win, for the web was always meant to ensnare us.

And as we fight, karma waits, watching us struggle in the very threads we wove, knowing that, in the end, it is not fate or chance that binds us, it is our own hands that created the entanglements, and only we can choose to break free. But first, we must realize that the struggle itself is the lesson, and the threads we are caught in are the consequences of our own making.

26. The Ripple Effect

A single drop of cruelty falls into the calm waters of the world, and in that instant, everything changes. At first, it seems like such a small act, almost imperceptible—a sharp word, a cold gesture, a selfish thought that manifests into action. But like the smallest stone tossed into a vast lake, it sends ripples across the surface, touching places far beyond where it first landed. The waves grow, moving outward, touching the edges of lives we may never know, creating disturbances that seem beyond our control.

We watch as the ripples spread, thinking the damage is done, the hurt has traveled far enough. Perhaps we think it won't reach us again. Perhaps we think that the far-off consequences are out of our grasp, a part of a world that exists separately from our own. But the ripples do not dissipate quietly. They always return.

For the shores, though seemingly distant, are never truly separate from the water. No matter how far the waves travel, they will always crash back to where they began. The cruelty we cast into the world does not fade into nothingness; it circles back, drawn by the unspoken law of balance, until it finds its way back to us. The harm we cause, the wounds we inflict—whether intentional or not—will one day return, just as the waves always return to the shore.

At first, we may not recognize the returning tide. It comes slowly, softly, as if the world is trying to teach us a lesson before we even notice it. But when the waves crash back against us, when the consequences of our actions are finally clear, we are reminded that no act, no matter how small, is ever truly without consequence. The ripple effect does not forget.

The shores may be patient, but they are not forgiving. The waves will always return, and we must face them. The drop of cruelty we once let fall into the water will one day come crashing back, forcing us to reckon with the ripples we've created.

27. Pendulum Swings

Life's pendulum moves with precision, its swing deliberate and unyielding. It arcs forward, propelled by forces both seen and unseen, each movement carving out its inevitable course. For every action we take, every choice we make, the pendulum swings, and the universe records it. We may feel we are at the center of the arc, unaffected by the forces that pull the pendulum back and forth, but the truth is that every swing has its counterbalance. Every force sent out into the world will eventually return with equal measure, whether we are ready for it or not.

When we act in cruelty, the pendulum swings toward harm, a sharp, unforgiving movement. We may think the pain we cause is fleeting, that it is forgotten by the time the swing reaches its farthest point. But time does not forget, and neither does the pendulum. It always returns. The harm we've set into motion is like the weight pulling the pendulum back, building its momentum, ready to strike once again. And when it does, the return is felt in ways we cannot escape— an equal measure of pain, regret, or consequence that finds its way back to its origin.

In the same way, the pendulum swings for acts of kindness and compassion. Though we may not see it in the moment, the goodness we offer to the world is carried by the pendulum, sending ripples outward. The swing of kindness may not always be as immediate or as obvious, but it moves with the same precision. And in time, it returns to us, just as forcefully as the swing of harm, though with gentler hands.

The pendulum does not judge. It does not choose who it favors or who it punishes. It simply moves with the laws of balance, ensuring that every action is met with a return. We cannot outrun it. We cannot escape its precision. What we send out will come back, and when the pendulum swings, we will feel the full force of its motion. Life's pendulum moves without mercy or hesitation, striking with equal measure, bringing us face to face with the consequences of our choices.

28. Hourglass of Retribution

The hourglass stands still, its sands slipping down grain by grain, almost imperceptible in their quiet descent. Each moment that passes, each small action, each choice made, is like a single grain of sand falling into the lower half. We go about our lives, unaware of the steady, silent passage of time, thinking that the consequences of our deeds will remain suspended, waiting for a moment that never seems to come. But just as the sands continue to fall, so too does the inevitable pull of retribution draw closer.

With every act, whether good or ill, the hourglass of retribution fills slowly, its contents unnoticed, as we move on, consumed by the present. We convince ourselves that we have time—that the things we've said or done, the promises broken, the wounds inflicted, are all lost in the sea of forgotten moments. But time is never truly forgotten. The grains slip, the sand falls, and what is set into motion will one day find its way back.

The moment of reckoning comes not with a roar or a warning, but with the quiet certainty of the sands running out. When the hourglass finally empties, the consequences are unavoidable. Retribution arrives with the weight of all the moments we didn't account for, all the harm we didn't think would come back. The time is up, and we are faced with what we've sown. No amount of denial or distraction can stop the inevitable. The hourglass has run out.

The moment of reckoning is not a matter of fate or chance; it is the natural law of time. The sands may fall slowly, but the truth is relentless. We can never outrun the final grains of the hourglass. Retribution will come when the time is right, as sure and certain as the falling sand. No matter how we try to stop it, no matter how we wish to delay it, the moment always arrives. The hourglass never forgets, and when it runs out, we are forced to face the consequences of what we've done.

29. Mirror of Time

Karma is not a distant force; it is a mirror, reflecting the true shape of our actions with unwavering precision. Each moment we live, each choice we make, becomes an imprint upon its surface, clear and undeniable. We may turn away from the mirror, convinced that the consequences of our deeds will fade with time, but the reflection remains. It waits patiently, forcing us to see the image we've created, one we cannot hide from, no matter how far we run.

In the mirror of time, there are no distortions. It does not soften the truth or blur the edges of our wrongs. When we hurt others, when we lie or betray, it shows us the faces of those we have wronged, their eyes filled with the pain we've caused. We are forced to meet their gaze, to see ourselves through their eyes, to feel the weight of what we've done. The mirror holds nothing back, offering a clear reflection of our actions, a reflection that refuses to be ignored.

Time does not erase what we've left behind. It only amplifies it, showing us the ripple effects of our choices, how they reverberate through the lives of those around us. The mirror of karma is not content with the surface-level view. It plunges deeper, forcing us to confront the scars we've inflicted, the trust we've shattered, the hearts we've broken. We cannot look away from the reflection; it forces us to face the consequences, to see ourselves as others see us.

In the end, we realize that karma is not some distant judge, but an ever-present witness to our actions. It gives us the chance to look at ourselves through the lens of time, to understand the truth of what we've done, and to reckon with the impact of our choices. The mirror does not lie. It shows us exactly who we are, and forces us to see, to feel, and to understand the lives we've touched—whether for good or ill.

30. Dancing Fates

Karma and Destiny move together, like dancers in perfect synchrony, their steps guided by an ancient, invisible rhythm. The stage is set, and the spotlight falls upon them, casting long shadows that stretch across time. At first, their movements are graceful, seemingly unhurried, as if they are simply performing their roles in a cosmic ballet. But beneath the surface, the dance is far more intricate, more deliberate than it appears. Each gesture, each twirl, is woven with meaning, and every step carries weight.

Karma leads with its sharp, unforgiving movements, each action met with a precise counter, an equal return. Every twist, every turn of the dance floor is a reflection of something sent into the world, each act of kindness or cruelty creating ripples that will eventually come back to the dancer. Destiny, ever the partner, follows with fluidity and grace, guiding the dance with the certainty of time itself. While Karma creates, Destiny steers, bringing events together in a way only it can predict. Neither can move without the other, and their movements intertwine in ways that feel inevitable, unavoidable.

As the dance unfolds, the steps quicken, the tempo rising, until the finale draws near. The dancers twirl faster now, their movements dizzying, their paths converging in a whirlwind of cause and effect. The audience watches, breathless, as the music swells, unaware that every choice, every misstep, every moment of hesitation has led them to this moment. The final curtain is near, and no one is spared. Not even the dancers themselves.

Karma's grip tightens, pulling the dancers together with a force neither can resist. There are no solos in this performance, no stars who shine brighter than the others. As the music nears its peak, the two forces collide—fates interwoven, actions and consequences entwined. The finale is not a grand, celebratory ending, but a culmination of everything that has come before. All must face the consequences of their roles in the dance. The floor is set, the music has played, and the final bow is taken.

In the end, there is no escaping the choreography. Karma and Destiny have danced together for eternity, their steps written into the fabric of the universe, and the finale spares no one. No one leaves the stage untouched.

(The Fall)

31. To the Days Before the Fall

Dear Yesterday,
I write to you from the edge of what was,
A place where memories linger like dust in the
air—
Soft, fleeting, yet impossible to ignore.
How simple the days once felt,
When the world was painted in hues of hope,
And laughter was a sound without echo.

Do you remember when time was kind?
When promises were just words we spoke with
ease,
And trust wasn't a fragile thing,
Fragile like glass waiting to shatter?
Oh, how I long to return to those moments,
Before the weight of the world became too much
And our hearts started to carry the scars
We never knew they would follow us.

In your arms, I knew peace,
The days before the descent into chaos,
Before the lies became truths
And the warmth turned cold.
I ask, in vain, to relive those moments—
To feel the sun's warmth without fear of it fading

*And the touch of a hand without the burden of
doubt.
But you, dear Yesterday, are just a shadow now,
A place I can never truly reach again.*

*You were once my refuge, my breath,
Now you are the ghost I chase
Through every sleepless night.
Your silence is a cruel reminder
Of the time lost to the winds of change.
I send this letter to you
Not because I expect a reply,
But because I need to say goodbye,
To mourn the days before it all unraveled.*

*Farewell, Yesterday.
May you rest in the corner of my heart
Where the past can never be erased—
Just remembered,
Forever remembered.*

32. The One who Watched Me Crumbled

Dear You,
I write this to the shadow that never spoke,
The silent witness to my unraveling.
You stood there, unmoving,
While I fell apart piece by piece,
Like glass slipping from my hands,
Breaking with every breath I took.
Did you feel the weight of my descent,
Or was your silence just easier than the truth?

You watched me crumble,
Saw the cracks that spread like wildfire
And said nothing,
As if I wasn't worth the effort
Of reaching out, of pulling me back.
I begged for help in whispers,
Hoping you might hear,
But you, too comfortable in your stillness,
Turned away when I needed you most.

Did you think I wouldn't notice
The absence of your voice,
The way you stayed silent,
When every ounce of my being screamed for
you to care?

You were a spectator,
An observer of my pain
But not the one who would lift me from it.
Did it hurt, watching me fall?
Did it bother you,
Or were you content to watch
As I disappeared under the weight of my own
breaking?

I used to believe you cared—
But now I see how easy it was for you to stay
Quietly safe in the distance,
Far from the mess I became.
You let me crumble,
Let me burn in my own fire,
And when I finally rose from the ashes,
You were nowhere to be found.

So here I stand,
A person made whole again,
Not by you, but in spite of you.
And though I'll never forget
The quiet betrayal in your stillness,
I've learned to live without you.
I've learned that sometimes,
The ones who claim to care
Are the very ones who watch us fall.

Goodbye,
To the one who watched me crumble.

33. Letter to Abyss

Dear Abyss,
I write to you from the edge of this chasm,
Where the light no longer reaches,
And the air is thick with silence.
You have always been there,
A constant shadow at my back,
Waiting, patient,
For the moment when I would stumble,
When I would fall
And allow you to swallow me whole.

I used to fight you,
Grasping at the last remnants of hope,
Foolishly thinking that I could outrun the darkness,
But now I know better.
You've become too familiar,
A weight on my chest that I can't shake off,
A voice in my head that whispers
That I am never enough,
That I am broken beyond repair.

How many times have I fallen to your embrace?
How many nights have I knelt before you,
Begging for release,

Only to find that your grip tightens,
That you thrive in my weakness?
You consume me slowly,
Filling the spaces where light once lived,
Turning every hope into dust
Until nothing is left but the hollow ache.

There is no escape,
I know this now,
And perhaps I never truly wanted one.
Perhaps I've grown too tired
Of pretending that there is a way out,
Too weary of the constant battle
That only seems to lead me back to you.
You have become a strange comfort,
The only thing that doesn't leave,
The only thing that never falters.

So here I am,
Confessing to you what I never dared to say—
I have surrendered.
I have accepted that I am yours,
That the darkness that now surrounds me
Is the only truth left to hold.
I am not afraid of you anymore,
For I know you better than I know myself.
We are one now,
Bound together in this endless night.

And yet, Abyss,
As I write this letter,
A small, foolish part of me still wonders—
Is there a piece of me that still wants the light?
Or have you consumed it all?

Yours,
A soul lost within the dark.

34. Fragile Future

Dear Future,
I write to you with trembling hands,
A heart full of questions that have no answers,
And a soul worn thin from the weight of what's
been lost.
You are all that's left now,
A faint glimmer in the distance,
Too distant to touch but too near to ignore.
I see you there,
Hoping, perhaps, to guide me out of this darkness,
But I'm unsure if I'm worthy of your light.
Do you remember me?
Do you still believe in me,
After all the choices I've made
That have led me to this shattered place?

I wonder if you, too, are fragile.
Like glass, I fear you'll break
With the first gust of wind,
With the first misstep I take on this uncertain
path.
Can I even walk toward you?
Or am I destined to wander,
A lost soul searching for something I no longer
understand?

Once, I thought I knew where you lay,
Once, I believed you were mine to claim,
But the fall has left me unrecognizable,
And I fear I have forgotten the way.
Each step feels like I am walking on air,
As if the ground beneath me could disappear
At any moment, leaving me to fall again.
But you—my Fragile Future—
You still whisper in the quiet,
A promise that things could be different,
If only I could find the courage
To hold onto you,
To trust that you won't slip through my fingers.

But how can I trust when so much has crumbled?
How can I believe when the past has taught me
That nothing is certain,
That even the brightest hopes can fade
Like stars swallowed by the night?
You are a delicate dream,
A fluttering butterfly that might never land,
But still, you remain,
Hanging by the thinnest thread.

So, I write to you now,
Not with certainty,
But with a quiet prayer that you stay.
That you hold on,
And that perhaps, in time,

I can learn to trust you again.
I don't know if I deserve you,
But I will keep reaching for you,
Even if I can barely see your outline
In the haze of my fear.

Yours,
A soul still searching for hope.

35. An Apology to Reflection

Dear Reflection,
I write this with a heavy heart,
Not knowing where to begin,
Or if I even deserve to address you anymore.
You, who once mirrored my strength,
Who knew the fire in my eyes
Before the world dimmed it,
Before I allowed myself to break.

I've forgotten who I was,
Or perhaps, I've simply let you slip away,
Fading into the shadows
As I lost sight of my own worth.
I no longer recognize the face I see when I look
at you.
The person staring back seems foreign,
A version of myself I no longer understand.
You've become a stranger,
And I wonder—
Have you always been there,
And I simply refused to see?

Once, I was sure of my path,
My voice was clear and strong,
But somewhere along the way,

I let the noise drown me out,
Let the doubts, the failures, the fears
Carve deep lines into who I was.
I let go of my power,
Piece by piece,
Until all I had left was a shadow
Of the person I used to be.

I am sorry, Reflection,
Sorry for abandoning you in the storm,
For letting the winds of doubt tear us apart.
I am sorry for believing the lies that told me
I wasn't enough,
That I had to shrink to fit into a world
That never understood me.
I am sorry for losing you
In the chaos of trying to be everything
For everyone else.

But now, I look at you with regret,
Wishing I could find the strength I once wore
Like armor,
Wishing I could see myself clearly again.
I long for the spark I know is buried deep inside,
For the fire that once burned bright and
unapologetic.
I promise, Reflection,
I will try to remember you,
To remember me.

I will search for the fragments of strength
That time has stolen,
And maybe, just maybe,
I will find my way back to you.

Yours,
A lost piece of myself.

36. Hands that pushed me

Dear Hands,
The ones that pushed me,
I write to you now,
Not with anger, but with the weight of all that's
been lost.
You, who once held me close,
Now the ones that shattered me
With a cruelty I never saw coming.
How easily you let go,
How swiftly you turned away
After the push that sent me falling,
Falling so far I almost forgot how to rise.

You didn't hesitate,
Didn't pause to consider
The consequences of your touch,
The one that sent me spiraling
Into a place where trust no longer exists.
Your hands, once tender,
Now the hands of betrayers,
Gripping tightly the lies you wove,
As you watched me break.

I wonder, as I lay here in the aftermath,
Did you know what you were doing?

Did you feel the weight of my fall
As your hands shoved me into the darkness?
Did it bring you satisfaction,
To watch the fragile foundation of my life
Crack under the force of your cruelty?
Or were you too blinded by your own selfishness
To see the destruction you caused?

I want to know,
Was it worth it?
Was it worth watching me crumble
To feel the power of your control
For a moment?
Did the pleasure of my pain
Make you forget the person you used to be,
The person I once trusted?

I may never understand
Why you chose to push me,
But I will remember,
Remember the hands that betrayed me,
And the fall that changed everything.
You cannot take back what you've done,
But know this—
I will rise again.
I will heal from the wounds you left behind.
And when I do,
I will remember the hands that pushed me,
Not with hatred,

But with the quiet understanding
That your cruelty was just another lesson
In a world that has taught me
How to survive without you.

Yours,
A soul that still stands.

37. A note from the Brink

Dear World,
I write to you from the edge,
Where everything feels suspended,
A moment stretched into eternity,
The calm before the storm,
The breath held just before the plunge.
I can feel the weight of this moment,
Heavy in the silence,
As if the universe itself is waiting
For me to take the final step.

I've stood here longer than I care to admit,
Watching the world blur in front of me,
A twisted reflection of all the things I should
have been,
Could have been,
But never became.
The choices I've made,
The ones I didn't,
The opportunities I missed,
They all gather around me now,
Like ghosts,
Whispering things I cannot undo.

There was a time when I thought
I could turn back,
When I believed there was still a way
To mend the cracks,
To rebuild what was broken.
But now, the edges feel too sharp,
The fall feels too inevitable.
I am standing on the precipice,
And the pull of gravity is stronger than hope.
There's no way to go but down,
No way to stop the world from spinning
Out of my control.

Do you see me here,
On the brink of something I can't name?
Do you understand that this is not a choice,
But a moment too heavy to carry any longer?
I once believed I could escape this—
The weight, the darkness, the doubt—
But now, all I feel is the cold,
The freezing grip of a future that I cannot face.
I wish I had the strength to step back,
To turn around and find another way,
But I'm here,
And this edge is the only thing that feels real.

So, I write this,
Not as a plea,
But as a confession.
This is where the road ends,
And the fall begins.
I've run out of words,
Out of hope,
Out of fight.
I am simply…
Standing.
Waiting.
And soon, I'll be gone.

Goodbye,
From the brink of the fall.

38. The Shadows I Became

Dear Remnants,
I write to you as someone I hardly recognize,
A ghost of who I was,
A shadow of the soul I once held so fiercely.
Do you remember me,
Before the light faded from my eyes?
Before the world began to blur,
And every color I once adored
Turned to shades of grey?

I wasn't always this way,
Wasn't always so lost in the dark.
Once, I was whole,
A vibrant burst of life and laughter,
A spirit untamed,
Chasing dreams with open arms.
But somewhere along the way,
I left myself behind,
Piece by piece,
Until all that was left
Were the fragments scattered in the shadows.

I feel you now,
The remnants of the person I used to be,
Haunting the corners of my mind,

A whisper of something beautiful,
Something I cannot quite touch.
How did I become this?
How did I let the world dim me,
Until I was no longer visible
Even to myself?

The shadows I became
Are not the kind that shelter you from the storm,
But the kind that swallow you whole,
The kind that cling to you
Like a second skin.
I wear them now,
These shadows that have become my home,
My only company,
While the soul I once was
Lingers just out of reach,
A memory fading with each passing day.

Do you remember the light?
Do you remember the fire that once burned so
brightly,
Before the weight of the world extinguished it?
I long to feel that warmth again,
To find the spark that would ignite me,
But all I have now
Are the echoes of who I was,
The shadows I've become,
And the emptiness that stretches between us.

I am sorry for letting you go,
For letting the light slip through my fingers,
For allowing myself to be consumed
By the darkness I once feared.
But here I stand,
A reflection of what remains,
A shadow of my former self,
And I wonder—
Can I find my way back to you?
Or is this all there is now?
The shadows.
The silence.
The remnants of a soul I once knew.

39. Letters Scattered in the Winds

Dear Unseen,
I write these words to you,
But I know you will never read them.
They will never find their way to you,
Lost in the wind,
Carried far away
Like thoughts that never quite take shape.
Perhaps this is the way it's meant to be,
The thoughts of the fallen,
Written, but never received.

I wonder if you ever thought of me,
In the moments before the silence fell.
Did you see me then,
When I was whole,
Before the cracks began to show,
Before the fall?
Or did you only see the person I became,
A shadow of myself,
Torn by regret and unanswered questions?

There are things I never said,
Words left unsaid,
Like letters scattered in the wind,
Carried away on gusts of lost chances.

I wanted to tell you then,
How much I loved,
How much I believed
That we could survive whatever storm came.
But I didn't speak,
I let the silence settle between us
Like a wall I couldn't climb.

I wish I had said more,
I wish I had been braver
In the moments when it mattered.
But the regrets I carry now
Are heavy,
Too heavy to put into words.
And so they float,
Like letters in the wind,
Unsent, unseen,
Floating away from me
Into a place where they can never return.
I wonder if you would have understood,
Would have seen me differently,
If only I had spoken my truth,
If only I hadn't let the fear of your silence
Drown my voice.
But the wind is unforgiving,
And the letters are gone,
Lost like the chances we never took.

So here I am,
Writing to you,
In a way I know will never reach you,
And in that, I find some kind of peace.
Because maybe,
Just maybe,
This is how it was meant to be—
The letters scattered in the wind,
A story told,
But never read.

Yours,
A voice that never found its way home.

40. The Stars I Can No Longer Reach

Dear Dreams,

I write to you with a heavy heart,
As one who once believed in the sky,
But now stands beneath it,
Shrouded in the shadow of what was never
meant to be.
I remember when you seemed so close,
When your light was within my grasp,
Shining like distant stars that whispered of
endless possibilities.
You were mine to chase,
Mine to hold,
But somewhere along the way,
I lost my way to you.

You were never too far,
Not until the fall began.
Not until I let the weight of the world pull me
under,
Until the dreams I once clung to
Became heavy burdens I could no longer carry.
I tried to reach for you,
I stretched my hands towards the heavens,
But the space between us only grew,

And the stars I once believed in
Became unreachable constellations,
Fading with every step I took away from who I
was.

I am sorry,
Sorry for letting go of you,
Sorry for the moment I stopped reaching.
But the climb was too steep,
And the weight of my fall was too great.
I wanted to keep reaching,
Wanted to believe you were still there,
Waiting for me to rise again.
But now, I see the truth,
The truth that I can no longer touch the stars
That once burned so brightly in my heart.

I leave you behind now,
Not because I want to,
But because I have no choice.
The descent has taught me that some things
Are meant to stay in the distance,
Things that I was never meant to hold,
Not with the hands that have become too tired,
Too broken,
To climb once more.

So this is my farewell,
To the stars I can no longer reach,
To the dreams that once defined me.
I'll carry you in my heart,
Even as I stand on earth,
Watching from below,
Knowing that though I cannot touch you,
I will always see you.
And perhaps, one day,
When the fall has finally stopped,
I'll learn to dream again.

Yours,
A soul that once reached for the sky.

Acknowledgments

This book would not have come to life without the unwavering support of one person—Wali Ahmad.

From the very beginning, you believed in this project when I had doubts, pushed me when I wanted to give up, and stood by me through every challenge.

Your constant encouragement and push made all the difference in making "The Lost - Betrayal, Karma, and Fall" a reality.

Thank you for always reminding me of my strength and pushing me to share my truth. Your belief in this work has been my foundation, and I am forever grateful.

To Wali, for everything.

As this collection comes to a close, I am reminded that the journey through betrayal, karma, and the fall is not a destination, but an ongoing process. Writing these poems was my way of navigating through moments of loss, regret, and reflection, and in doing so, I discovered that every fall is a chance for a new beginning.

Each poem in this book represents a moment in time, an emotion, a realisation, or a lesson learned. The themes of betrayal and karma are not just abstract concepts; they are lived experiences that shape us, challenge us, and ultimately, help us grow. As much as these poems reflect the pain and sorrow that comes with these experiences, they also speak to the resilience of the human spirit and the quiet strength that emerges from the ashes.

I hope this collection resonates with anyone who has faced betrayal, felt the sting of consequences, or found themselves at the bottom, unsure of how to rise again. We all have our moments of doubt, our moments of fall, but it is in those moments that we truly discover who we are and what we are capable of.

To everyone who has walked this journey with me through these pages, thank you for reading, for reflecting, and for allowing these words to become part of your own journey. The stories within these poems are yours as much as they are mine.